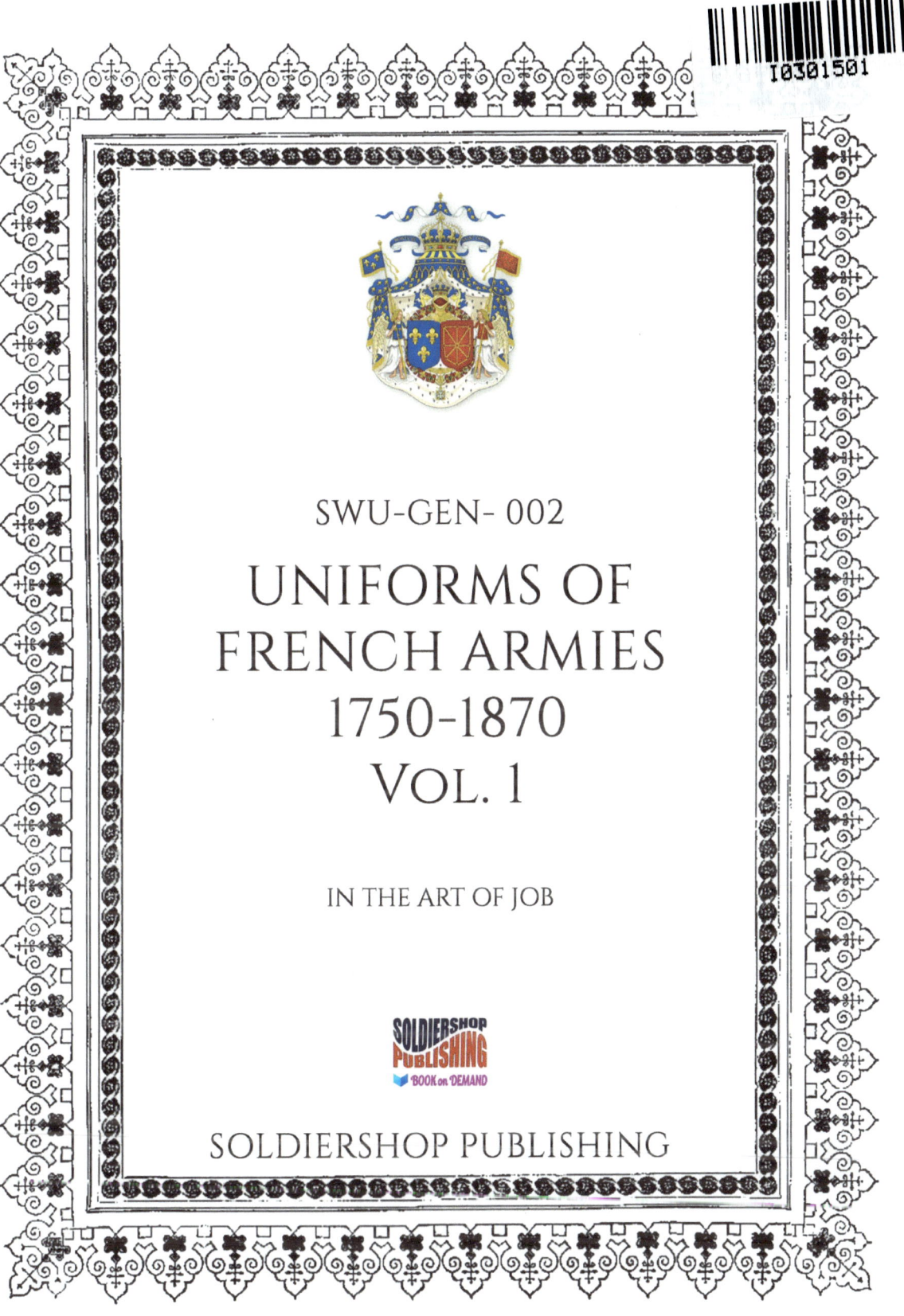

SWU-GEN- 002

UNIFORMS OF FRENCH ARMIES 1750-1870 VOL. 1

IN THE ART OF JOB

SOLDIERSHOP PUBLISHING

AUTHOR

Jacques Marie Gaston Onfroy de Bréville, known by the pen name **Job** after his initials (25 November 1858, Bar-le-Duc – 15 September 1931, Neuilly-sur-Seine) was a famous French artist and illustrator that maintained a keen taste for military, patriotic and nationalistic subjects.

PUBLISHING'S NOTE

None of **unpublished** images or text of our book may be reproduced in any format without the expressed written permission of Soldiershop.com when not indicate as marked with license creative commons 3.0 or 4.0. The publisher remains to disposition of the possible having right for all the doubtful sources images or not identifies. Our trademark: Soldiershop Publishing ©, The names of our series: Soldiers&Weapons, Battlefield, War in colour, PaperSoldiers, Soldiershop e-book etc. are herein © by Soldiershop.com.

NOTE ABOUT BOOK PRINTING BEFORE 1925

This book may contain text or images coming from a reproduction of a book published before 1925 (over seventy years ago). No effort has been made to modernize or standardize the spelling used in the original text, so this book may have occasional imperfections such as missing or blurred pages, poor pictures, errant marks, etc. that were either part of the original artifact, or were introduced by the scanning process. We believe this work is culturally important, and despite the imperfections, have elected to bring it back into print (digital and/or paper) as part of our continuing commitment to the preservation of printed works worldwide. We appreciate your understanding of the imperfections in the preservation process, and hope you enjoy this valuable book. Now this book is purpose re-built and is proof-read and re-type set from the original to provide an outstanding experience of reflowing text, also for an ebook reader. However Soldiershop publishing added, enriched, revised and overhauled the text, images, etc. of the cover and the book. Therefore, the job is now to all intents and purposes a derivative work, and the added, new and original parts of the book are the copyright of Soldiershop. On this second unpublished part of the book none of images or text may be reproduced in any format without the expressed written permission of Soldiershop. Almost many of the images of our books and prints are taken from original first edition prints or books that are no longer in copyright and are therefore public domain. We have been a specialized bookstore for a long time so we (and several friends antiquarian booksellers) have readily available a lot of ancient, historical and illustrated books not in copyright. Each of our prints, art designs or illustrations is either our own creation, or a fully digitally restoration by our computer artists, or non copyrighted images. All of our prints are "tagged" with a registered digital copyright. Soldiershop remains to disposition of the possible having right for all the doubtful sources images or not identifies.

LICENSES COMMONS

Much of the text in this book are from the *"Memoirs of the Empress Catherine II., by Catherine II, Empress of Russia"* This book is for the use of anyone anywhere at no cost and with almost no restrictions whatsoever. You may copy it, give it away or re-use it under the terms of the similar creative commons License. This book may utilize material marked with license creative commons 3.0 or 4.0 (CC BY 4.0), (CC BY-ND 4.0), (CC BY-SA 4.0) or (CC0 1.0). We give appropriate attribution credit and indicate if change were made below in the acknowledgements field.

ACKNOWLEDGEMENTS

A Special Thanks to NYPL and other institutions for their kindly permission to use some images of his archives, collections or books used in our book.

Title: **UNIFORMS OF FRENCH ARMIES 1750-1870 VOL. 1 - IN THE ART OF JOB**
By Luca Stefano Cristini, color plates by Job. Serie edit by Luca S. Cristini. First edition by Soldiershop. July 2019
Cover & Art Design: Luca S. Cristini. ISBN code: 978-88-93274340
Published by Luca Cristini Editore, via Orio 35/4- 24050 Zanica (BG) ITALY. www.soldiershop.com

UNIFORMS OF FRENCH ARMIES 1750-1870 Vol. 1

THE REVOLUTIONARY ARMY IN THE ART OF JOB

Luca Stefano Cristini

THE WONDERFUL WORLD OF THE JOB'S SOLDIERS

In this book are present the development and complexity of France's uniforms, from the Louis XV era just to Second Empire of Napoleon III. All the subjects are seen through the eyes of a great French artist. Jacques Marie Gaston Onfroy de Bréville, well known by the pen name Job after his initials (1858-1931).
The serie is published on 3 volume that includes about 200 and more wonderful original illustrations of uniforms from the 18th century to Napoleonic era and just to 1870 about.
This book presents pictorial documentation of the appearance of French soldiers throughout the period with the support of short essays on France's military history. The particularly well-executed original Job's illustrations, slightly restored by our graphic artist are presented to the general public here for the first time. Job's plates shows how the Royal and (after) Imperial French Army, time and again, was a decisive factor in the story of Europe.

In the first volume of the serie we present the French soldiers from Ancien Regime just to revolutionary years.

IL MERAVIGLIOSO MONDO DEI SOLDATI DI JOB

In questo libro presentiamo il fascino e la storia delle uniformi francesi, dalle armate di Luigi XV a Napoleone III e il Secondo Impero. Tutti soggetti sono opera di un solo grande artista: Jacques Marie Gaston Onfroy de Bréville (1858-1931), meglio noto con lo pseudonimo di Job, dalle iniziali del suo nome. Tutte le tavole fanno parte di una collezione di oltre duecento disegni a colori, e sono presentati su tre volumi. Si tratta come è noto del periodo più glorioso della storia di Francia, e la maestria di Job , fervente patriota oltre che grande artista, rende particolare merito a queste tavole capolavoro. Questo lavoro è anche il primo mai edito in Italia.
In questo primo volume sono trattate le uniformi dell'Ancien regime fino all'avventura rivoluzionaria che darà vita negli anni a venire alla epica era napoleonica. Buona lettura e soprattutto buona visione

Portrait of Louis XV, King of France (1710-1774) paint by Louis Michel Vanloo (1707-1771)

SHORT HISTORY OF THE FRENCH ARMY

THE FRENCH SOLDIER OF ANCIEN RÉGIME

The French Renaissance and the beginning of the *Ancien Régime*, normally marked by the reign of Francis I, saw the nation become far more unified under the monarch. The power of the nobles was diminished as a national army was created. With England expelled from the continent and being consumed by the Wars of the Roses, France's main rival was the Holy Roman Empire. This threat to France became alarming in 1516 when Charles V became the king of Spain, and grew worse when Charles was also elected Holy Roman Emperor in 1519. France was all but surrounded as Germany, Spain, and the Low Countries were controlled by the Habsburgs. The lengthy Italian Wars that took place during this period resulted in defeat for France and established Catholic Spain, which formed a branch of the Habsburg holdings, as the most powerful nation in Europe. Later in the 16th century, France was weakened internally by the Wars of Religion. As nobles managed to raise their own private armies, these conflicts between Huguenots and Catholics all but demolished centralization and monarchical authority, precluding France from remaining a powerful force in European affairs. On the battlefield, the religious conflicts highlighted the influence of the gendarmes, heavy cavalry units that comprised the majority of cavalrymen attached to the main field armies. The pride of the royal cavalry, gendarme companies were often attached to the main royal army in hopes of inflicting a decisive defeat on Huguenot forces, although secondary detachments were also used for scouting and intercepting enemy troops.

After the Wars of Religion, France could do little to challenge the dominance of the Holy Roman Empire, although the empire itself faced several problems. From the east it was severely endangered by the Ottoman Empire, with which France formed an alliance. The vast Habsburg empire also proved impossible to manage effectively, and the crown was soon divided between the Spanish and Austrian holdings. In 1568, the Dutch declared independence, launching a war that would last for decades and would illustrate the weaknesses of Habsburg power. In the 17th century, the religious violence that had beset France a century earlier began to tear the empire apart. At first France sat on the sidelines, but under Cardinal Richelieu it saw an opportunity to advance its own interests at the expense of the Habsburgs. Despite France's staunch Catholicism, it intervened on the side of the Protestants. The Thirty Years' War was long and extremely bloody, but France and its allies came out victorious. After their victory, France emerged as the sole dominant European power under the reign of Louis XIV. In parallel, French explorers, such as Jacques Cartier or Samuel de Champlain, claimed lands in the Americas for France, paving the way for the expansion of the French colonial empire.

The long reign of Louis XIV saw a series of conflicts: the War of Devolution, the Franco-Dutch War, the War of the Reunions, the Nine Years War, and the War of the Spanish Succession. Few of these wars were either clear victories or definite defeats, but French borders expanded steadily anyway. The west bank of the Rhine, much of the Spanish Netherlands, and a good deal of Luxembourg were annexed while the War of the Spanish Succession saw the grandson of Louis placed on the throne of Spain. The French strategic situation, however, changed decisively with the Glorious Revolution in England, which replaced a pro-French king with an enemy of Louis, the Dutch William of Orange. After a period of two centuries seeing only rare hostilities with France, England now became a consistent enemy again, and remained so until the 19th century. To stop French advances, England formed coalitions with several other European powers, most notably the Habsburgs. While these armies had difficulties against the French on land, the British Royal Navy dominated the seas, and France lost many of its colonial holdings. The British economy also became Europe's most powerful, and British money funded the campaigns of their continental allies.

Wars in this era consisted mostly of sieges and movements that were rarely decisive, prompting the French

military engineer Vauban to design an intricate network of fortifications for the defense of France. The armies of Louis XIV were some of the most impressive in French history, their quality reflecting militaristic as well political developments. In the mid-17th century, royal power reasserted itself and the army became a tool through which the King could wield authority, replacing older systems of mercenary units and the private forces of recalcitrant nobles. Military administration also made gigantic progress as food supply, clothing, equipment, and armaments were provided in a regularity never before equaled. In fact, the French embedded this standardization by becoming the first army to give their soldiers national uniforms in the 1680s and 1690s. The 18th century saw France remain the dominant power in Europe, but begin to falter largely because of internal problems. The country engaged in a long series of wars, such as the War of the Quadruple Alliance, the War of the Polish Succession, and the War of the Austrian Succession, but these conflicts gained France little. Meanwhile, Britain's power steadily increased, and a new force, Prussia, became a major threat. This change in the balance of power led to the Diplomatic Revolution of 1756, when France and the Habsburgs forged an alliance after centuries of animosity. This alliance proved less than effective in the Seven Years' War, but in the American Revolutionary War, the French helped inflict a major defeat on the British.
See also: List of Ancien Régime wars and battles

FRENCH REVOLUTIONARY WARS

The armies of the Revolution at Jemappes in 1792. With chaos internally and enemies on the borders, the French were in a jittery state in 1792. By 1797, however, they had exported their ideology (and the army that followed it) to the Low Countries and Northern Italy. The French Revolution, true to its name, revolutionized nearly all aspects of French and European life. The powerful sociopolitical forces unleashed by a people seeking liberté, égalité, and fraternité made certain that even warfare was not spared this upheaval. 18th-century armies—with their rigid protocols, static operational strategy, unenthusiastic soldiers, and aristocratic officer classes—underwent massive remodeling as the French monarchy and nobility gave way to liberal assemblies obsessed with external threats. The fundamental shifts in warfare that occurred during the period have prompted scholars to identify the era as the beginning of "modern war".

In 1791 the Legislative Assembly passed the "Drill-Book" legislation, implementing a series of infantry doctrines created by French theorists because of their defeat by the Prussians in the Seven Years' War. The new developments hoped to exploit the intrinsic bravery of the French soldier, made even more powerful by the explosive nationalist forces of the Revolution. The changes also placed a faith on the ordinary soldier that would be completely unacceptable in earlier times; French troops were expected to harass the enemy and remain loyal enough to not desert, a benefit other Ancien Régime armies did not have. Following the declaration of war in 1792, an imposing array of enemies converging on French borders prompted the government in Paris to adopt radical measures. August 23, 1793, would become a historic day in military history; on that date the National Convention called a levée en masse, or mass conscription, for the first time in human history. By summer of the following year, conscription made some 500,000 men available for service and the French began to deal blows to their European enemies.

Armies during the Revolution became noticeably larger than their Holy Roman counterparts, and combined with the new enthusiasm of the troops, the tactical and strategic opportunities became profound. By 1797 the French had defeated the First Coalition, occupied the Low Countries, the west bank of the Rhine, and Northern Italy, objectives which had defied the Valois and Bourbon dynasties for centuries. Unsatisfied with the results, many European powers formed a Second Coalition, but by 1801 this too had been decisively beaten. Another key aspect of French success was the changes wrought in the officer classes. Traditionally, European armies left major command positions to those who could be trusted, namely, the aristocracy. The hectic nature of the French Revolution, however, tore apart France's old army, meaning new men were required to become officers and commanders.

Besides opening a flood of tactical and strategic opportunities, the Revolutionary Wars also laid the foundation for modern military theory. Later authors that wrote about "nations in arms" drew inspiration from the French Revolution, in which dire circumstances seemingly mobilized the entire French nation for war and incorporated nationalism into the fabric of military history. Although the reality of war in the France of 1795 would be different from that in the France of 1915, conceptions and mentalities of war evolved significantly. Clausewitz correctly analyzed the Revolutionary and Napoleonic eras to give posterity a thorough and complete theory of war that emphasized struggles between nations occurring everywhere, from the battlefield to the legislative assemblies, and to the very way that people think. War now emerged as a vast panorama of physical and psychological forces heading for victory or defeat.

THE ARTIS JOB

Jacques Marie Gaston Onfroy de Bréville, known by the pen name **Job** after his initials (25 November 1858, Bar-le-Duc – 15 September 1931, Neuilly-sur-Seine) was a French artist and illustrator. His father opposed his entry to thé École des beaux-arts after graduating from the Collège Stanislas. He therefore joined the French army, but returned to Paris in 1882. In the intervening period, he maintained a keen taste for military, patriotic and nationalistic subjects. He finally joined the École des beaux-arts and exhibited at the 1886 'Salon des artistes français', receiving a mixed reception. He therefore began a career as an illustrator, contributing caricatures to *La Caricature* and to *La Lune*. However, he is best known for his illustrations for children's books, most frequently for texts by Georges Montorgueil. His major colour compositions contributed to the cult of 'heroes of the nation' such as Napoleon I and Joachim Murat. Several of his illustrations appear in *La Vieille Garde impériale* (*The Old Imperial Guard*), published in 1932 by Alfred Mame and fils de Tours. His eye for detail can be seen in *L'Épopée du costume militaire français* - even in works intended for children, he tried to reproduce uniforms with extreme precision.

Job pencil self portrait

His best known works are *Murat, Le Grand Napoléon des petits enfants, Jouons à l'histoire, Louis XI, Napoléon, Bonaparte* and *Les Gourmandises de Charlotte*. He also illustrated the life of George Washington and was well known in the USA. He was a Sociétaire of the 'humoristes' and exhibited with the Incoherents. His studio has been reconstructed at the musée de Metz

French carrying the British redoubts at Yorktown, 1781, by Job.

THE PLATES
Vol. 1

1759 Dragoons of Regt. Beauffremont

1760 Draft outfits for the King's Regiment - Drummers

PROJET DE TENUES POUR LE RÉGIMENT DU ROI
FIFRE ET MUSICIEN

1760 Draft outfits for the King's Regiment - Flute and trumpet

GARDE FRANÇAISE
(TELS QU'ILS FONT L'EXERCICE EN ÉTÉ

1760 French guard in summer dress

Bonnet de police d'officier du Régiment de l'Hospital-Dragons
(1725-1739).

Casque de la légion de Lorraine.
(Cavalerie.)

Casque du colonel Lataye.

1725-1739 Bonnet de police of Hospital dragon Regt., 1769-1775 Lorraine cavalry legion helmet, 1794 Colonel Lataye's helmet

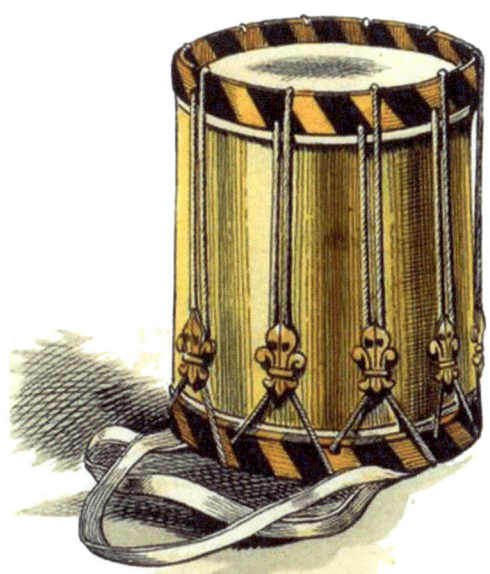

Tambour des gardes lorraines (1750).

Giberne d'officier d'infanterie, règne de Louis XV.
(Grandeur de l'objet 18 centimètres 1/2 sur 13 centimètres.)

1750 Lorraine guard drum, 1765 Infantry gibern under Louis XV

CAPITAINE DE DRAGONS DE LA LÉGION DE CONDÉ
CI-DEVANT VOLONTAIRES ÉTRANGERS DE CLERMONT-PRINCE
Copie d'un portrait à l'huile fait a Cleves le 1er Mai 1762
(Collection de M. G. Cottreau)

1762 Captain of dragoons from Condé legion

TAMBOUR DES GARDES FRANÇAISES (RÈGNE DE LOUIS XV).

1763 French guard drum under Louis XV

1765-1775 Grenadier of infantry Regt. Orleans

1766 Corsican legion soldiers: carpenter and sapper

1769-1775 Corsican legion uniforms

1770 Draft outfits for the King's Regt.: colonel's flag and battalion flag

1770 Draft outfits for the King's Regt.: rifleman, sergeant and grenadier officer

1770 French grenadier

SERGENT DU RÉGIMENT DE BAYONNE (1772).

1772 Sergeant of Bayonne Regt.

1773 Details of the armament and equipment of the Corsican legion

1774 Drum of the Anhalt Regt. in Strasbourg

LE PRINCE DE NASSAU-SIEGEN

D'après une miniature appartenant à M. G. Cottreau.

1778 Prince of Nassau Siegen

1781 Trumpets of dragoon Regt. Orleans

1784 Colonel of the Chamborant hussars

DRAGONS
DES MILICES DE SAINT-DOMINGUE SOUS LOUIS XVI

1786 Dragoons trooper of San Domingo militia

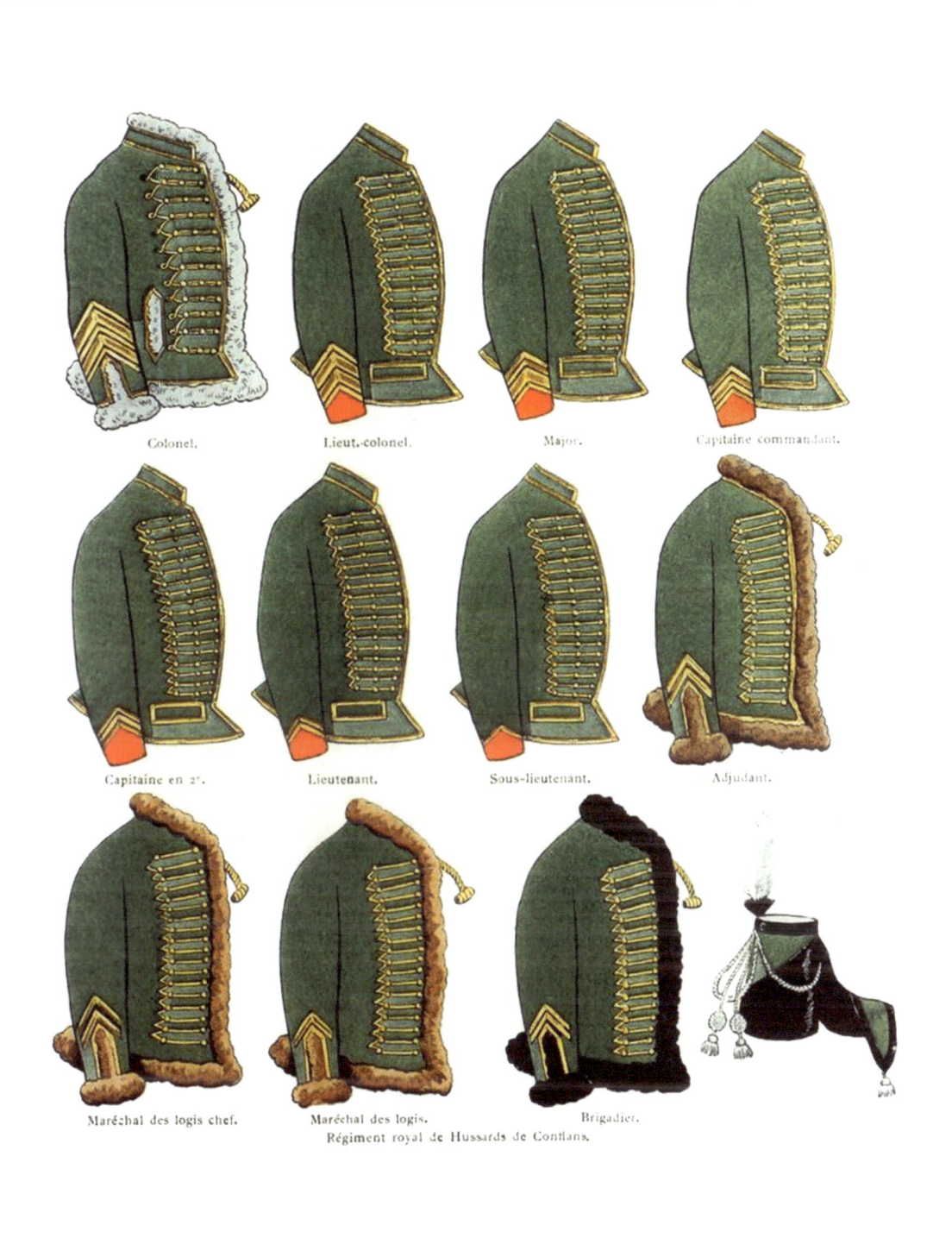

1786 Royal Regt. of hussars of Conflans

1786-1788 Military school uniforms

GARDE FRANÇAISE DU DÉPÔT.

1787 French guard of the warehouse

OFFICIER DE LA CONNÉTABLIE (EN GRAND UNIFORME)

1787 Officer of the Connéttablie

1787 Officer of the Connéttablie (in short uniform)

INFANTERIE ET ARTILLERIE
DE LA GARDE NATIONALE DE NANTES
(1789-1790)

1789 Artillery and infantry of Nantes national guards

CAPORAL DES CENT-SUISSES EN HABIT DE CÉRÉMONIE

1789 Corporal of the Cent-Suisse in ceremonial dress

FIFRE DU REGIMENT DES GARDES SUISSES EN PETITE TENUE

1789 Musician of the Swiss guard Regt. in short uniform

MUSICIEN DES GARDES SUISSES, TENUE DE VERSAILLES SOUS LOUIS XVI

1789 Musician of the Swiss guard Regt. in Versailles uniform

TROMPETTE DE HUSSARDS DE CONFLANS DEVENUS HUSSARDS DE SAXE

1789 Trumpet of the Saxon hussars

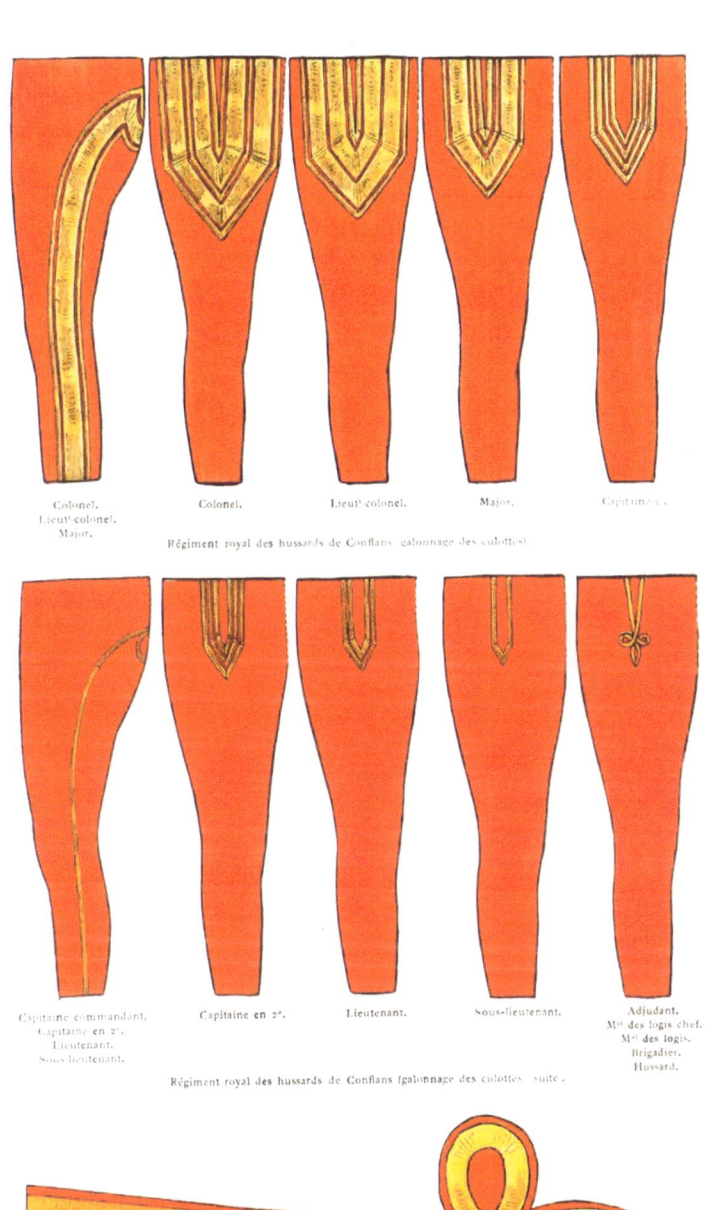

1786-1789 Details of hussar officers and brigadiers of Conflans

Ornement de retroussis d'officier de volontaires (époque de la Révolution).
Ces ornements de retroussis sont tirés du carnet d'échantillons d'un passementier du commencement de la Révolution.
Ce précieux document fait partie de la Collection de M. Cottreau.

Ornement de retroussis d'habit (commencement de la Révolution).
(Collection G. Cottreau.)

Tambour de la Révolution (Collection de M. Job).
(Les ondes à la Suisse semblent indiquer un tambour de la République Helvétique.)

1789-1790 Ornaments and drum of the Revolution

Mirliton de Hussards
(1ʳᵉ République)

Habit journalier des officiers de hussards de Conflans

SCHAKO DU 7ᵉ HUSSARDS
(CONSULAT)

1786-1799 Uniforms, mirliton and shako of hussar of Conflans and 1ˢᵗ Republic

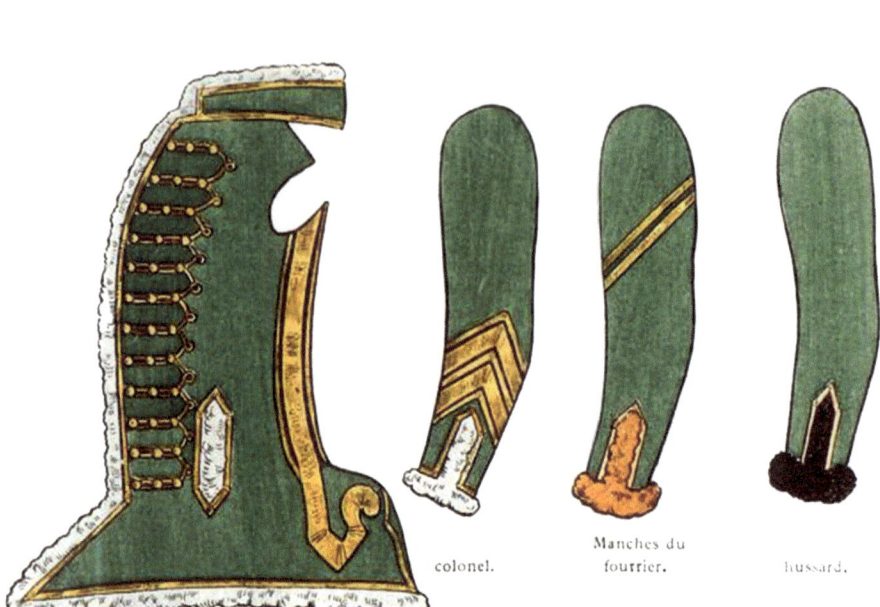

Coupe de la pelisse du colonel. — colonel. — Manches du fourrier. — hussard.

Régiment royal des Hussards de Conflans. (Galon large, galon étroit, cordonnet, dimensions réelles.)

1786-1792 Royal Regt. of the hussars of Conflans

1790 Grenadier of infantry Regt. of Berwick

GRENADIER DU RÉGIMENT COLONEL-GÉNÉRAL. INFANTERIE

(1790)

1790 Grenadier of infantry Regt. of lieutenat general

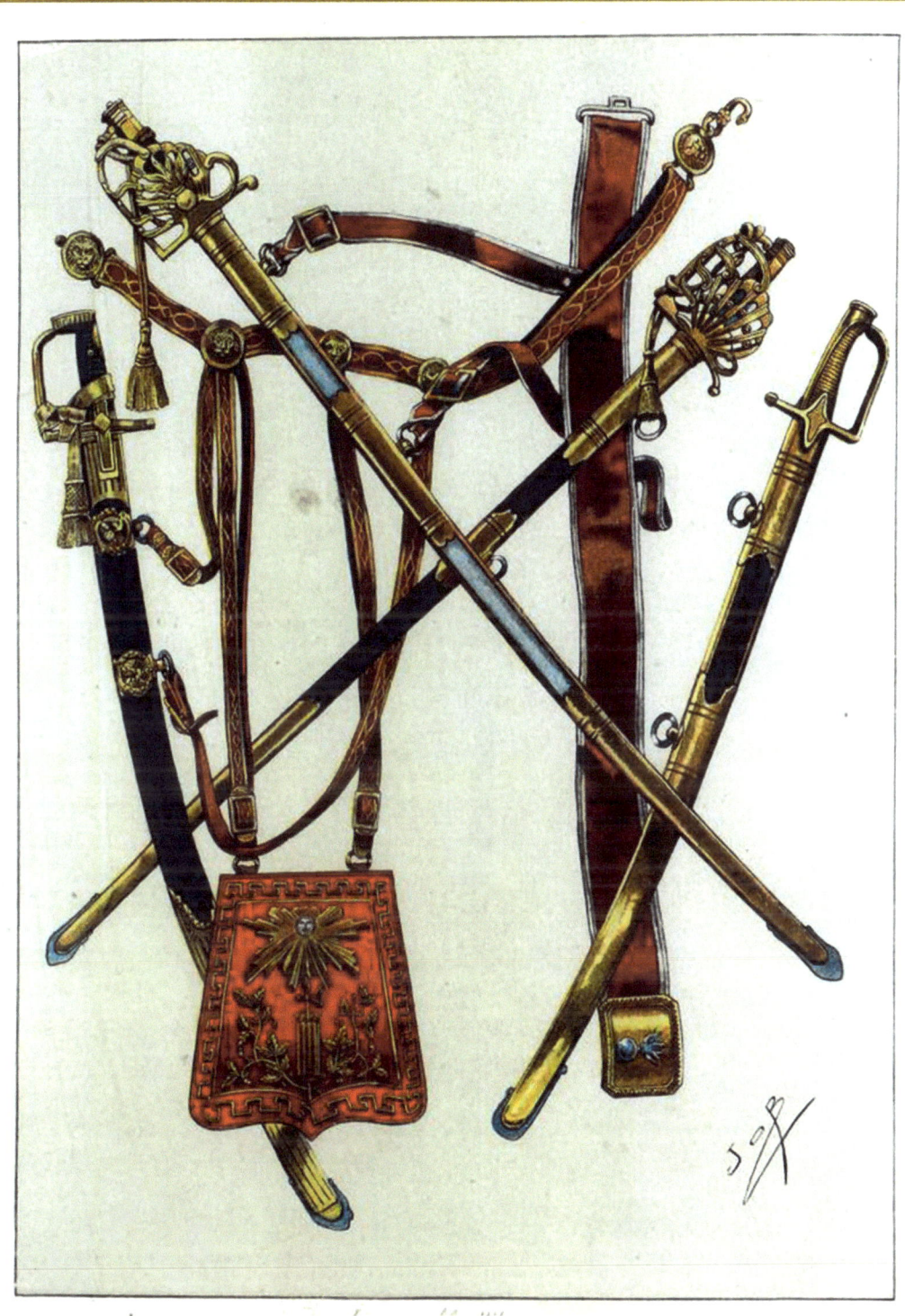

1789-1815 Cavalry officers' swords

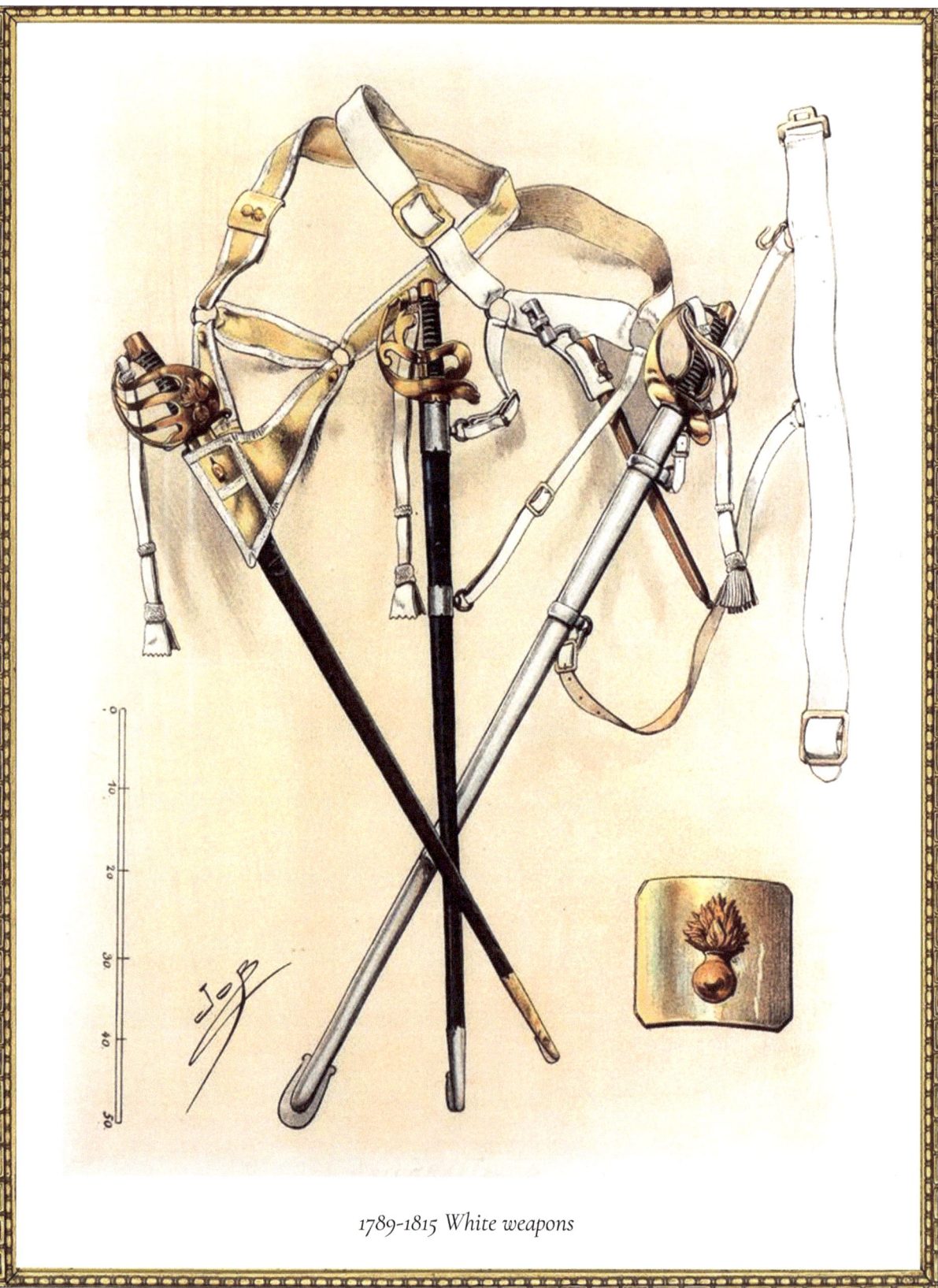

1789-1815 White weapons

CHASSEUR DES BARRIÈRES DE PARIS (1790).

1790 Paris barrier chasseur

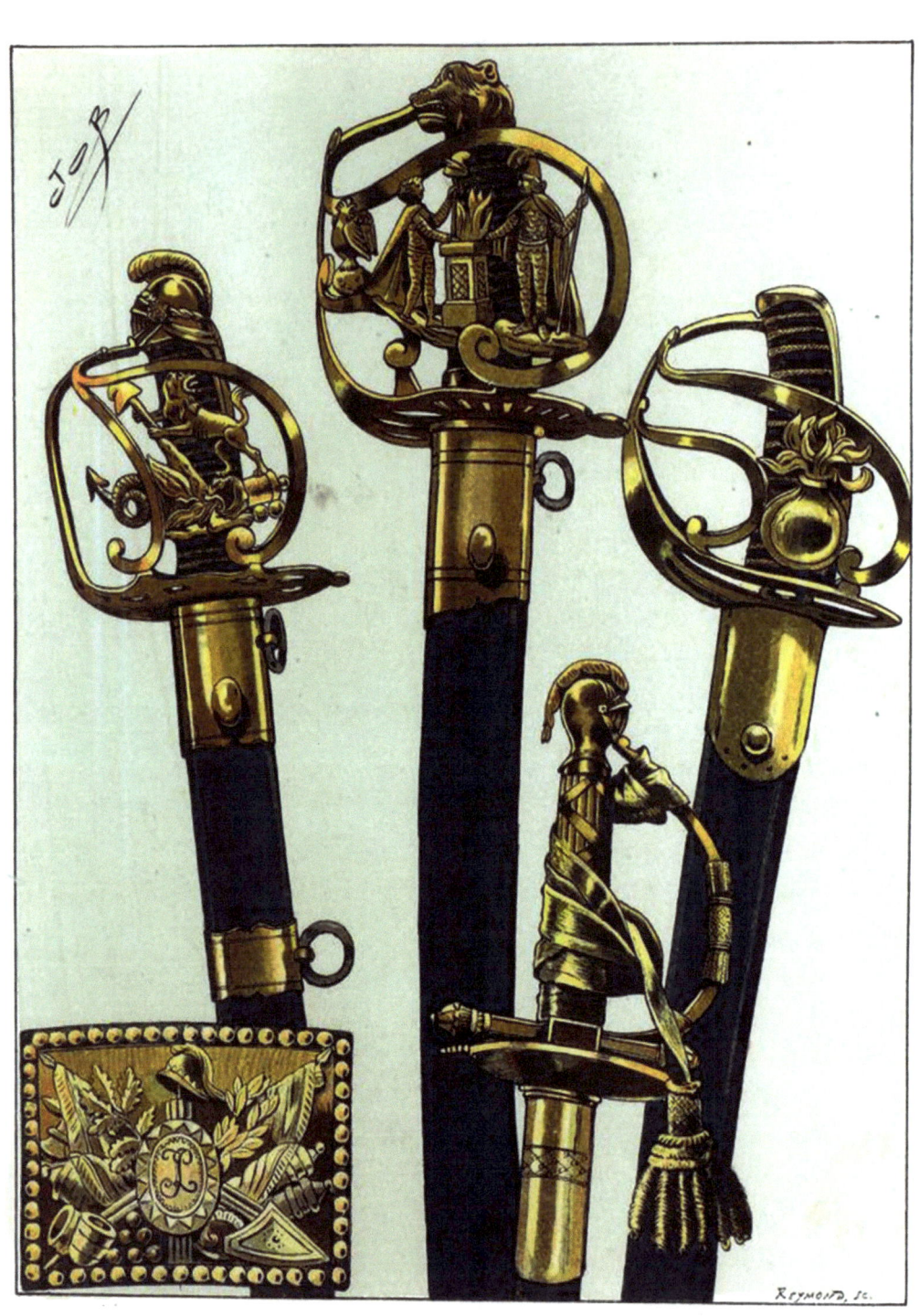

1790 Revolution swords

1790 Soldier and cannonier of the Swiss guards under Louis XVI

1790 Toulon national guards

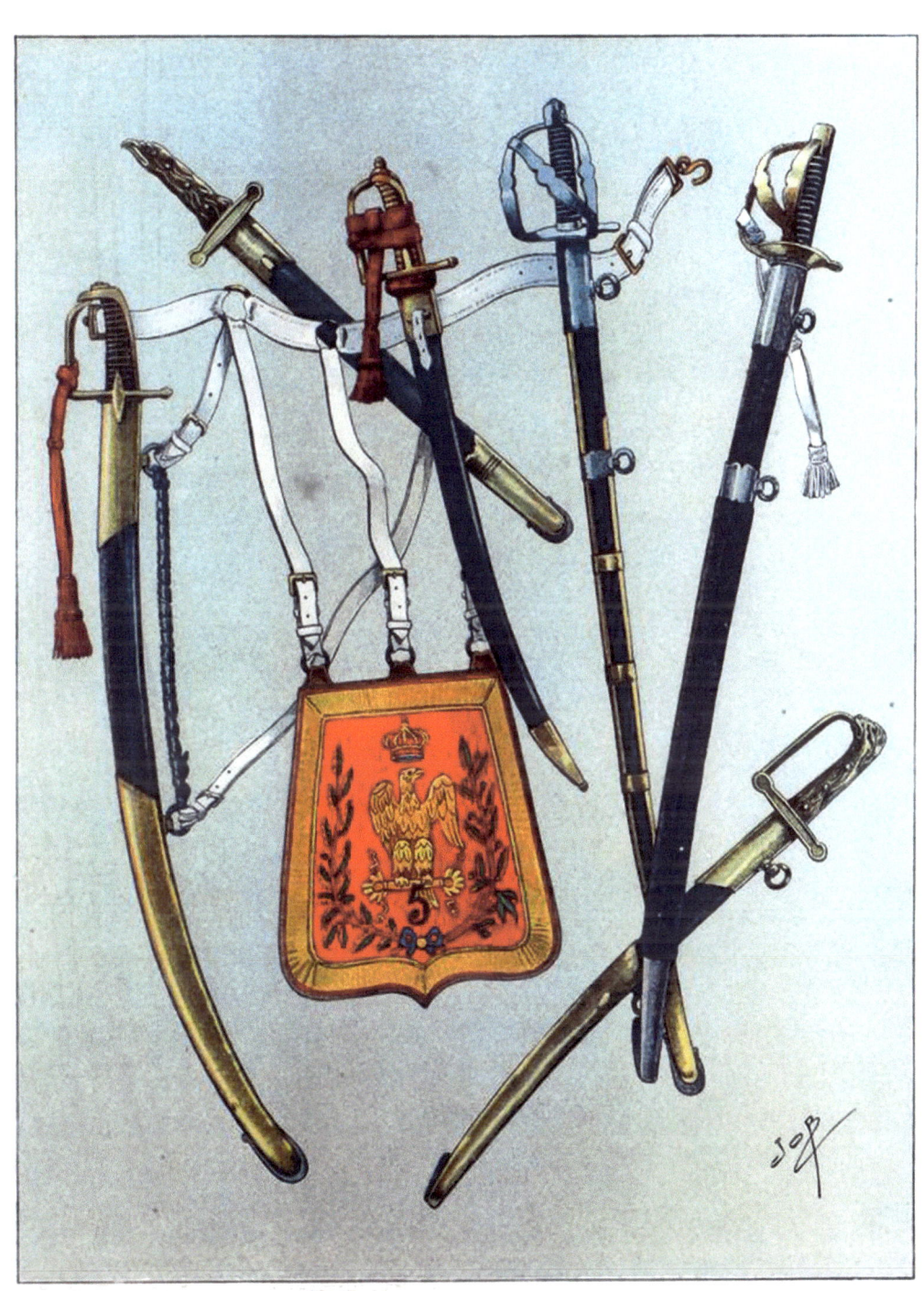

1790 Troop swords

1790-1810 Trumpet of carabiniers

TROMPETTE D'ARTILLERIE A CHEVAL (1792)

1792 Trumpet of horse artillery

Portrait de François Pie, grenadier du 74ᵉ Régiment de ligne (1792). (D'après un dessin du Cabinet des Estampes à la Bibliothèque Nationale.)

1792 Portrait of François Pie, grenadier of the 74th line Regt.

OFFICIER DE VOLONTAIRES (HIVER DE 1792 A 1793).

1792-1731 Volunteers' officer

1793 Fusilier of the Basque company of Bayonne

OFFICIER DE MARINE 1793
(D'après une miniature du temps, Collection de M. Job.)

1793 Navy officer

1793 Strasbourg pontonniers

1793 Vendéen horseman and horse pricker, or piconnier, of the Germanic legion

1794 Hussars and trumpet during the Revolution

CHASSEUR DE DAMAS

1795 Chasseaur of the Damas legion

1795 Hussar of the Damas legion

1796 1st French legion

MÉDARD BONNARD, CAPORAL FOURRIER A LA 105ᵉ DEMI-BRIGADE, 1796.

1796 Médard Bonnard, corporal fourrier to the 105th half-brigade

1798 9th half-brigade battle in Egypt

9ᵉ DEMI-BRIGADE DE LIGNE

TAMBOUR MAJOR (PETIT UNIFORME) TENUE D'ÉGYPTE.

MUSICIEN (PETIT UNIFORME) AN X.

1799 9th infantry half-brigade in Egypt: major drum and musician

UNE CANTINIÈRE (ÉPOQUE DE LA RÉVOLUTION).

1799 Canteen lady during the Revolution

CHAPEAU CHINOIS DE LA 57ᵉ DEMI-BRIGADE EN 1799

1799 Chinese hat of the 57th half-brigade

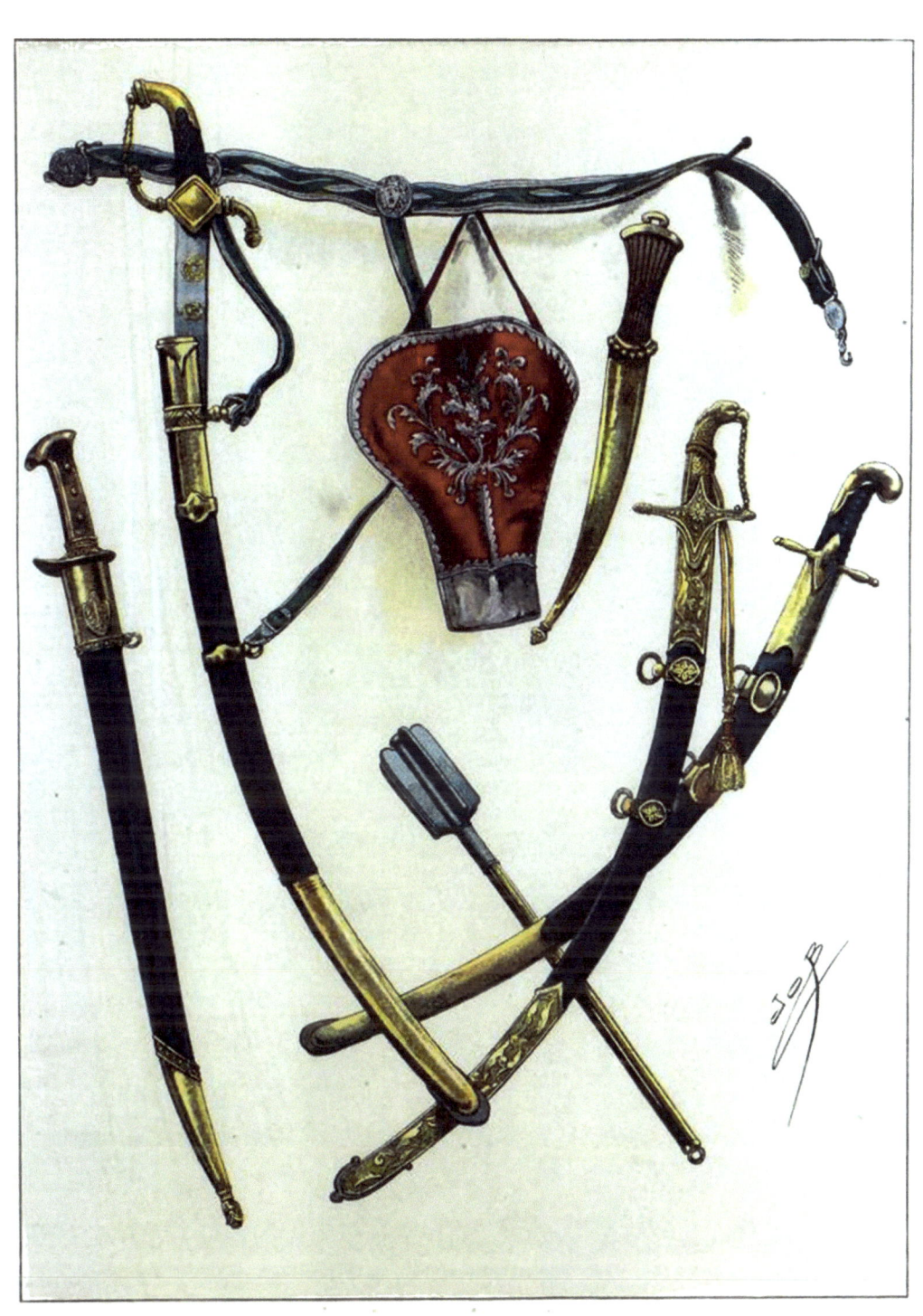

1799 Eastern weapons

OFFICIER ET DRAGON DU 5ᵉ RÉGIMENT EN TENUE DE VILLE (TENUE D'HIVER, CONSULAT).

1799 Officer and dragoon of the 5th Regt. in street clothes

OFFICIER DE CAVALERIE DE LA LÉGION POLONAISE (1799).

1799 Cavalry officer of Polish legion

TAMBOUR-MAJOR ET MUSICIEN D'INFANTERIE LÉGÈRE (1800)

1800 Drum major, drum and light infantry musician

TRAIN D'ARTILLERIE (AN VIII)

1800 Artillery gear

RÉGIMENT DES DROMADAIRES. ARMÉE D'ÉGYPTE (1801).

1801 Camel Regt., Egyptian Army

CHEF DE MUSIQUE DE LA GARDE DU GÉNÉRAL EN CHEF A SAINT-DOMINGUE (1802)

1802 Musician of the commander guard in Saint Domingo

1759-1775 Weapons and equipment of dragoon and grenadier

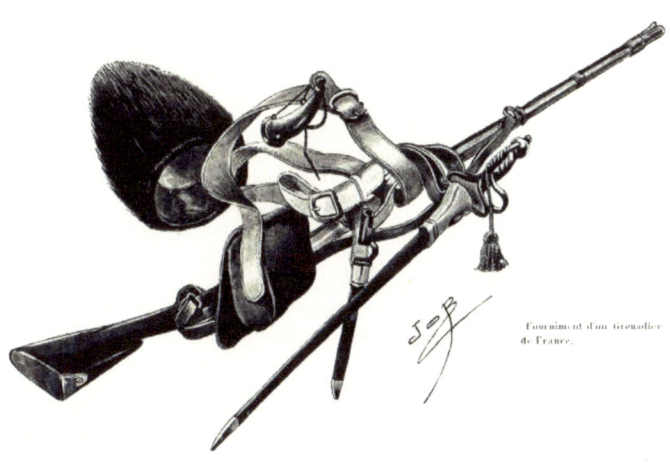

Fourniment d'un Grenadier de France.

Pistolet matricule 1777, dit à coffre.

Sabre du Royal Allemand.

1770-1780 Weapons and equipment of cavalry and grenadier

1790-1801 Revolutionary weapons and equipment, headgear and flag

French cavalry in the XVIII century

SOLDIERS, WEAPONS & UNIFORMS ALREADY PUBLISHED
(SOME TITLES)

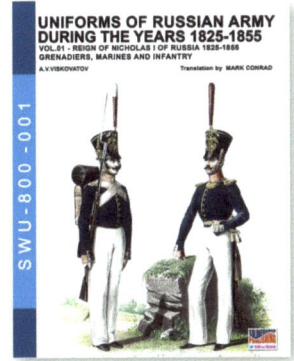
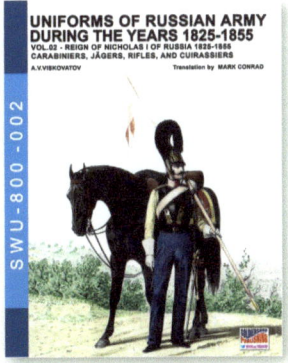
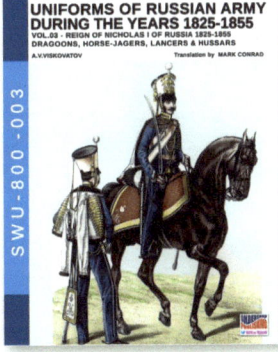
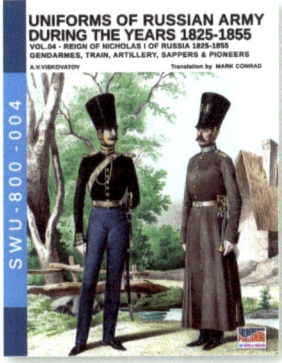
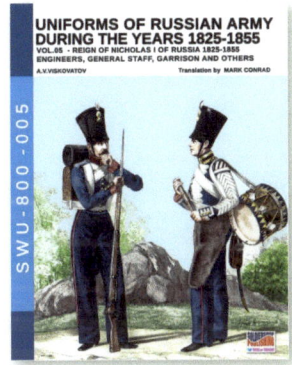
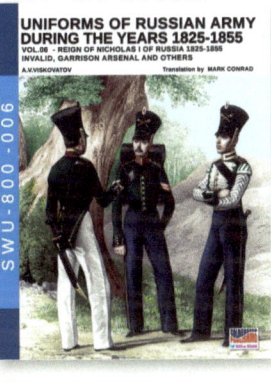
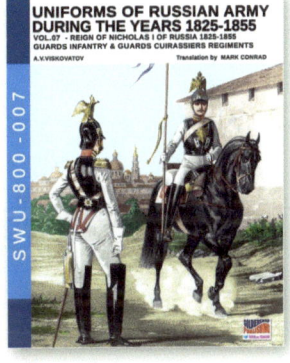
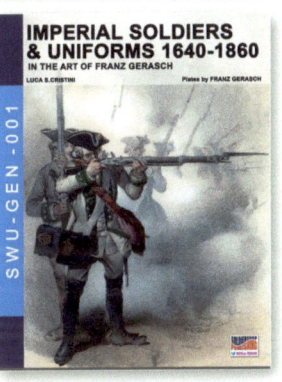
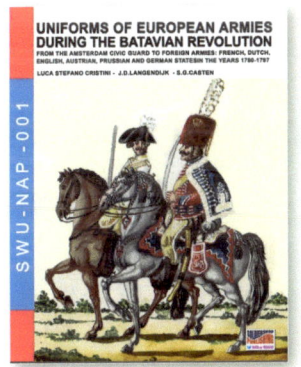
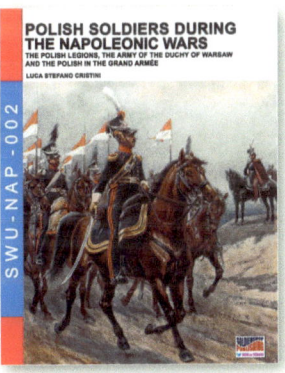

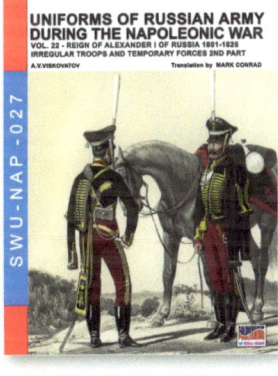
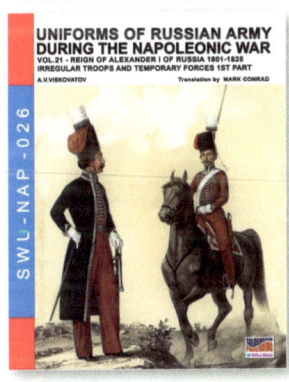
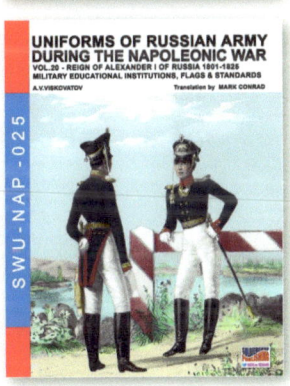
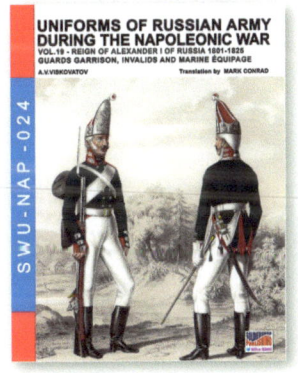
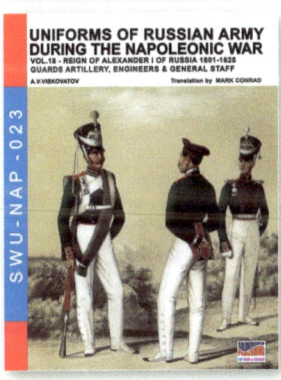

www.ingramcontent.com/pod-product-compliance
Lightning Source LLC
Chambersburg PA
CBHW041524220426
43669CB00003B/38